BRIGHT
IDEA
BOOKS

DWAYNE
Johnson

by Samantha S. Bell

CAPSTONE PRESS

a capstone imprint

Bright Idea Books are published by Capstone Press
1710 Roe Crest Drive, North Mankato, Minnesota 56003
www.mycapstone.com

Library of Congress Cataloging-in-Publication Data
Library of Congress Cataloging-in-Publication Data is available on the Library of Congress
website.
ISBN: 978-1-5435-5794-7 (library hardcover)
978-1-5435-6039-8 (paperback)
978-1-5435-5826-5 (eBook PDF)

Editorial Credits
Editor: Claire Vanden Branden
Designer: Becky Daum
Production Specialist: Colleen McLaren

Photo Credits
Alamy: Adam Scull, 16–17; AP Images: Alan Diaz, 13, Jordan Strauss/Invision, cover; Newscom:
Mavrixonline.com, 18; Rex Features: Dave Allocca/Star Pix, 20, Sony/Moviestore, 6–7; Shutterstock
Images: Everett Collection, 9, Kathy Hutchins, 5, 15, 23, 26, 28, Shawn Goldberg, 30–31,
Tinseltown, 24–25; Yearbook Library: Seth Poppel, 10

Printed in the United States of America.
PA48

TABLE OF CONTENTS

CHAPTER 1

AT THE Top

Dwayne Johnson is tall and strong.

He has a big smile. He is a good listener.

He likes connecting with people.

Johnson is a movie star. He had a lead **role** in the movie *Jumanji: Welcome to the Jungle* in 2017. Four high school students play an old video game in the movie. Each one chooses an **avatar**. The students are sent into the game. They become the avatars. Johnson plays the strong hero.

Dwayne Johnson was the second-highest paid actor in 2017. He made $65 million that year.

Jumanji was a very successful film. Many directors want Johnson to be in their movies. He can play many different roles. He is easy to work with and coach. Johnson is one of the highest paid actors in the United States.

6

Johnson works hard. He is thankful for the people who help and support him.

CHAPTER 2

FOOTBALL
Star

Johnson was born on May 2, 1972. He is **biracial**. His father is African-Canadian. His mother is **Samoan**.

Johnson's father was a wrestler. The family moved a lot. They did not have much money. Johnson changed schools many times.

Before Johnson became a big movie star, his family struggled to afford rent and food.

Johnson (left) used to arm wrestle his classmates in high school.

Johnson hung out with a bad crowd as a teenager. He caused trouble in school. He fought and stole. He was arrested many times.

Then Johnson met Coach Jody Cwik. Cwik told Johnson to join the high school football team. Everything changed for Johnson. He worked very hard. He earned a football **scholarship** for college.

HARD TIMES

Johnson went to the University of Miami. He was a star player his first year. Then he was hurt. A player named Warren Sapp took his place. Sapp was even better than Johnson.

Johnson wanted to join the National Football League after college. Sapp was picked. But no teams wanted Johnson. He joined a Canadian football team instead. After two months, he was cut from the team. Johnson left his football career with just seven dollars.

Dwayne "The Rock" Johnson &
Dany Garcia Johnson

October 2 _20_ _07_

PAY TO THE
ORDER OF _____ U aTHLET

One Million Dollars

Football Facilities Renovation

Johnson did not make it in football, but he was thankful for his time at Miami. He later gifted the school $1 million.

DIFFICULT DAYS

Johnson was very sad when he left football. He struggled with **depression** for many years.

CHAPTER 3

WRESTLING Star

Johnson's father is Rocky Johnson.
He was one of the first black **tag team**
wrestling champions. Johnson's grandfather
was Peter Maivia. He was one of the first
Samoan wrestlers. Johnson wanted to try
wrestling too. His father agreed to train him.

Johnson joined the World Wrestling Federation in 1996. He called himself Rocky Maivia. He soon won his first championship.

Johnson is very close to his parents, Ata and Rocky.

Johnson (right) wrestled against Chris Jericho in 1999.

Johnson was often smiling. He wanted to win over the crowd. But the crowd booed him instead. He was still new. People didn't like him yet.

Then Johnson got hurt. He stopped wrestling for a while. He thought about why fans might not like him. He was not being himself. He was not being real with the fans.

Every once in awhile, Johnson comes back to his wrestling roots.

THE ROCK

Johnson decided to change his image. There are heroes and villains in professional wrestling. This gives the audience someone to root for. It makes for a good show.

Johnson came back to wrestling as a villain. He became the Rock. He enjoyed the crowd's reactions. He could connect with them. He was a fan favorite within a month.

Johnson went from winning wrestling championships to starring in movies.

Johnson went on to win eight World Wrestling Entertainment (WWE) Championships. He still remembers the lesson he learned. He believes the most powerful thing you can be is yourself.

THE PEOPLE'S EYEBROW

The Rock had a famous look. He raised one eyebrow. He lowered the other. He called it "the People's Eyebrow."

CHAPTER 4

MOVIE Star

Johnson was at the top in wrestling.

He had accomplished many things.

It was time for a new challenge. He wanted

to reach more people. He decided to

start acting.

Johnson knew he had a lot to learn about acting. He wanted to know everything about making movies. **Directing** and **producing** interested him too.

On December 13, 2017, Johnson received his star on the Hollywood Walk of Fame.

Johnson's first major movie was in 2001. He played the Scorpion King in *The Mummy Returns*. He has made many more movies since then. These include action films such as *Fast Five*. He has also made family films such as *Moana*.

Johnson starred in *Moana* with Auli'i Cravalho. The movie made more than $600 million.

Johnson has been with his longtime girlfriend Lauren Hashian for more than 10 years.

Johnson likes to tell people his story. He worked hard at football. But he did not accomplish that dream. Then he tried something else. He didn't give up. Now he is a success. He wants people to know they can reach their dreams too.

THE BEST JOB

Johnson has three daughters. He believes his most important job is being a father.

GLOSSARY

avatar
a figure representing a certain person in a video game

biracial
having parents of two different races

depression
a very sad state

direct
to control the artistic aspects of a movie

produce
to guide the creation of a movie from start to finish, including developing a script, hiring the director, and overseeing the budget

role
a part played by an actor

Samoan
someone from Samoa, an island in the South Pacific

scholarship
money given to a student to help pay for further education

tag team
a team of two or more wrestlers who take turns fighting in the ring

28

TIMELINE

1972: Dwayne Johnson is born.

1995: Johnson graduates from the University of Miami.

1996: Johnson starts his wrestling career.

2001: Johnson stars in his first major movie, *The Mummy Returns*.

2016: Johnson voices Maui in the super successful family film *Moana*.

2017: Johnson has one of the leading roles in *Jumanji: Welcome to the Jungle*.

ACTIVITY

MAKE AN ACTION MOVIE

Get together with friends or family members to make your own action movie!

First, decide what the movie is about. An action movie usually includes a hero and a villain. Then, decide what other characters you will need and write a script. Assign a role to each person acting in the movie. Then gather any costumes or props you will use.

Now for the fun part! Act out the scenes as someone films with a smartphone or tablet. When you are finished, share and show your movie! You may choose to edit it first with an app or computer program.

FURTHER RESOURCES

Want to know more about the WWE? Check out these books:

Black, Jake. *The Ultimate Guide to WWE*. New York: Grosset & Dunlap, 2011.

Miller, Dean, and Steven Pantaleo. *WWE: Absolutely Everything You Need to Know*. New York: DK Publishing, 2017.

Orr, Tamra. *Day by Day with Dwayne "The Rock" Johnson*. Hockessin, DE: Mitchell Lane Publishers, 2012.

Interested in acting and moviemaking? Check out some of these resources:

Stoller, Bryan Michael. *Smartphone Movie Maker*. Somerville, Mass.: Candlewick Press, 2017.

Young, Rebecca. *102 Monologues for Middle School Actors*. Colorado Springs, CO: Meriwether Pub. Ltd., 2012.

INDEX